John Rutter

Choral Works

for TTBB choirs

OXFORD

OXFORD
UNIVERSITY PRESS

Great Clarendon Street, Oxford OX2 6DP,
United Kingdom

Oxford University Press is a department of the University of Oxford.
It furthers the University's objective of excellence in research, scholarship,
and education by publishing worldwide. Oxford is a registered trade mark of
Oxford University Press in the UK and in certain other countries

This collection © Oxford University Press 2022

John Rutter has asserted his right under the Copyright, Designs
and Patents Act, 1988, to be identified as the Composer of these Works

First published 2022

Impression: 1

All rights reserved. No part of this publication may be reproduced,
stored in a retrieval system, or transmitted, in any form or by any means,
without the prior permission in writing of Oxford University Press

Permission to perform the works in this anthology in public
(except in the course of divine worship) should normally be obtained from
a local performing right licensing organization, unless the owner or the occupier
of the premises being used already holds a licence from such an organization.
Likewise, permission to make and exploit a recording of these works
should be obtained from a local mechanical copyright licensing organization

Enquiries concerning reproduction outside the scope of the above
should be directed to the Music Rights Department, Oxford University Press, at
music.permissions.uk@oup.com or at the address above

ISBN 978–0–19–356102–1

Music originated on Sibelius
Printed in Great Britain on acid-free paper by
Halstan & Co. Ltd, Amersham, Bucks.

Contents

A Gaelic Blessing	4
Blow, blow, thou winter wind	9
Candlelight Carol	19
God be in my head	29
Lead, kindly Light	32
Nativity Carol	34
O waly, waly	41
The Lord bless you and keep you	47
When the saints go marching in	54

A Gaelic Blessing

William Sharp (1855–1905)
adapted by JR

JOHN RUTTER

*The signs ⌐ ¬ denote the melody line, when it is not in the top voice.

The organ accompaniment to the mixed-voice version is compatible with the voice parts of this TTBB version.

© 1978, 1995, 2020 The Royal School of Church Music. Reprinted by permission.

9
peace to you, Deep peace of the
peace to you, Deep peace of the
air to you, Deep peace of the qui-et
peace to you, Deep peace of the
13
mp
earth to you, Deep peace of the
mf
earth to you, Deep peace of the shin-ing
(mp)
earth to you, Deep peace of the
mp
earth to you, Deep peace of the
mp

17
(mp)
stars to you, Deep peace of the gen-tle
p
stars to you, Deep peace of
p
stars to you, Deep peace of
p
stars to you, Deep peace of
p
21
mf
night to you, Moon and stars pour their heal-ing
mp
night to you, Moon and stars pour their
mp
night to you, Moon and stars pour
mp
night to you, Moon and stars pour
mp

25
p
light on you, Deep peace of
(mp)
light on you, Deep peace of
p
light on you, Deep peace of
p
light on you, Deep peace of
p
29
cresc.
mf cresc.
Christ, of Christ the
cresc.
mf cresc.
Christ, of Christ the
cresc.
mf cresc.
Christ, of Christ, of Christ the
cresc.
mf cresc.
Christ, of Christ the
cresc.
mf cresc.

33
f
dim.
light of the world to you,
light of the world to you,
light of the world to you,
light of the world to you,
37
mp
dim.
rall.
pp
Deep peace of Christ to you.
Deep peace of Christ to you.
Deep peace of Christ to you.
Deep peace of Christ to you.

Blow, blow, thou winter wind

Words by William Shakespeare

JOHN RUTTER

The original version, for mixed choir, is also published (ISBN 978-0-19-340552-3). The present arrangement is compatible with the composer's orchestration (2 flutes, harp, harpsichord, strings).

© Oxford University Press 1975. This arrangement © 2021.

Printed in Great Britain

OXFORD UNIVERSITY PRESS MUSIC DEPARTMENT, GREAT CLARENDON STREET, OXFORD OX2 6DP

The Moral Rights of the Composer have been asserted. Photocopying this copyright material is ILLEGAL.

21
B.
man's in-gra-ti - tude, as man's in - gra - ti -
26
TENORS 1 and 2
A
unis.
mp
dolce espress.
T.
Thy tooth is not so keen, Be -
B.
-tude;
A
31
T.
-cause thou art not seen, Al - though thy breath be
35
rude, al - though thy breath be rude.

39
B
p legato
T. 1
Heigh ho! sing, heigh ho! un - to the green
T. 2
Heigh ho! sing, heigh ho! un - to the green
B. 1
Heigh ho! sing, heigh ho! un - to the green
B. 2
Heigh ho! sing, heigh ho! un - to the green
Fls.
p
44
cresc.
mf
hol-ly: Most friend - ship is feign - ing, most lov - - - ing mere
hol-ly: Most friend - ship is feign - ing, most lov - - - ing mere
hol-ly: Most friend - ship is feign - ing, most lov - - ing mere
hol-ly: Most friend - ship is feign - ing, most lov - - ing mere

* The signs ⌐ ¬ denote the melody line, when it is not in the top voice.

59
C
C
Hpschd.
mp
65
D
mp
Ah
mp
Ah
mf ma dolce e legato
Freeze, freeze, thou
mf ma dolce e legato
Freeze, freeze, thou
D
Fl./Hp.
mf
Ped.

69
ah
ah
ah
bit - ter- sky,
freeze,
freeze,
thou
bit - ter- sky,
freeze,
freeze,
thou
Ped.
Ped.
Ped.
74
ah
ah
ah
ah
bit - ter- sky,
That dost not bite so nigh As
bit - ter- sky,
That dost not bite so nigh As
sim.

79
ah
ah
ah
ah
be - ne-fits for - got,
as be - ne - fits
for -
be - ne-fits for - got,
as be - ne - fits
for -
84
mf
E
Though thou the wa-ters warp, Thy sting is not so
mf
Though thou the wa-ters warp, Thy sting is not so
mp
- got:
Ah
ah
mp
- got:
Ah
ah
E
mp

89
mf
sharp
As
sharp
As friend re - mem-ber'd not, as
cresc.
ah
mf
ah
cresc.
93
F
(mf)
friend re - mem-ber'd not.
Heigh ho! sing,
(mf)
friend re - mem-ber'd not.
Heigh ho! sing,
mf
(mf)
ah
Heigh ho!
(mf)
Heigh ho!
F
mf
Ped.

98
heigh ho! un - to the green hol - ly: Friend - ship is
heigh ho! un - to the green hol - ly: Most friend - ship is
sing, heigh ho! un - to the green hol - ly: Most friend - ship is
sing, heigh ho! un - to the green hol - ly: Friend - ship is
103
feign - ing, lov - - ing mere fol - ly:
feign - ing, most lov - - - - ing mere fol - ly:
feign - ing, most lov - - - - ing mere fol - ly:
feign - ing, lov - - ing mere fol - ly:
dim.
Ped.

107
mp
p
Then, heigh ho, the hol-ly! This
Then, heigh ho, the hol-ly! This
Then, heigh ho, the hol-ly! This
Then, heigh ho, the hol-ly! This
(dim.)
mp
dim.
112
poco rall.
life is most jol-ly.
life is most jol-ly.
life is most jol-ly.
life is most jol-ly.
poco rall.
Hpschd.
p
dim.
pp

Candlelight Carol

Words and music by
JOHN RUTTER

*If the accompaniment is played on the piano, some notes in the left-hand chords will need to be omitted.

This carol is available in its original version for mixed voices (ISBN 978-019-340738-1) and also for upper voices (978-019-353365-3).

© Oxford University Press 1985. This arrangement © 2022.

* The signs ⌐ ¬ denote the melody line, when it is not in the top voice.

26
f
cra - dle till break-ing of dawn. Glo-ri - a, glo-ri - a
f
cra - dle till break-ing of dawn. Glo - ri - a, glo-ri - a
f
cra - dle till break-ing of dawn. Glo-ri - a, glo-ri - a
f
cra - dle till break-ing of dawn. Glo-ri - a, glo-ri - a
Sw.
mf
31
mp
p
in ex-cel - sis De - o! An - gels are sing - ing; the Christ child is born.
mp
p
in ex-cel - sis De - o! An - gels are sing - ing; the Christ child is born.
mp
p
in ex-cel-sis De - o! An - gels are sing - ing; the Christ child is born.
mp
p
in ex-cel - sis De - o! An - gels are sing - ing; the Christ child is born.
Ch.
p

*or other vocalized sound, such as 'Oo', at conductor's discretion.

48
cresc.
mf
dim.
p
Na - tions pro - claim him their Lord and their Sa - viour, But
Na - tions pro - claim him their Lord and their Sa - viour, But
keep; Ah
keep; Ah
Hum
53
C
p molto legato
Ma - ry will hold him and sing him to sleep. Can - dle -
Ma - ry will hold him and sing him to sleep. Can - dle -
Hum
Can- dle-light,
Can-dle-light,

58
cresc.
-light, an-gel light and star - glow Shine on his cra - dle till
cresc.
-light, an-gel light and star - glow Shine on his cra - dle till
cresc.
an-gel light, fire - light and star - glow Shine on his cra - dle till
cresc.
an-gel light, fire - light and star - glow Shine on his cra - dle till
cresc.
63
f
break-ing of dawn. Glo-ri - a, glo-ri - a in ex-cel - sis
f
break-ing of dawn. Glo - ri - a, glo-ri - a in ex-cel - sis
f
break-ing of dawn. Glo-ri - a, glo-ri - a in ex-cel-sis
f
break-ing of dawn. Glo-ri - a, glo-ri - a in ex-cel - sis
Sw.
mf

68
mp
p
De - o! An - gels are sing - ing; the Christ child is born.
De - o! An - gels are sing - ing; the Christ child is born.
De - o! An - gels are sing - ing; the Christ child is born.
De - o! An - gels are sing - ing; the Christ child is born.
Ch.
(Ch.)
73
D
Hum
3. Find him at Beth - le - hem laid in a

78
man - ger: Christ our Re - deem - er a - sleep in the hay,
83
mf cresc.
f
p
God-head in - car - nate and hope of sal - va - tion: Hum
mf cresc.
f
p
God-head in - car - nate and hope of sal - va - tion: Hum
mf cresc.
f
p
God-head in - car - nate and hope of sal - va - tion: A child with his
mf cresc.
f
p
God-head in - car - nate and hope of sal - va - tion: Hum
Sw. p
Man.

88
E
p molto dolce
Can-dle-light, an-gel light,
p molto dolce
Can-dle-light, an-gel light,
p molto dolce
mo-ther that first Christ-mas Day.
Can-dle-light, an-gel light,
p molto dolce
Can-dle-light, an-gel light,
E
Ch.
Ped.
93
fire-light and star-glow Shine on his cra-dle till break-ing of
fire-light and star-glow Shine on his cra-dle till break-ing of
fire-light and star-glow Shine on his cra-dle till break-ing of
fire-light and star-glow Shine on his cra-dle till break-ing of

98
f
dawn. Glo-ri-a, glo-ri-a in ex-cel-sis De-o!
f
dawn. Glo-ri-a, glo-ri-a in ex-cel-sis De-o!
f
dawn. Glo-ri-a, glo-ri-a in ex-cel-sis De-o!
f
dawn. Glo-ri-a, glo-ri-a in ex-cel-sis De-o!
Sw.
cresc.
f
103
mp
rall.
dim.
p
An-gels are sing-ing; the Christ child is born.
mp
dim.
p
An-gels are sing-ing; the Christ child is born.
mp
dim.
p
An-gels are sing-ing; the Christ child is born.
mp
dim.
p
An-gels are sing-ing; the Christ child is born.
rall.
Ch.
p

God be in my head

Words from the Sarum Primer (1514)

JOHN RUTTER

*The signs ⌐ ¬ denote the melody line, when it is not in the top voice.

Also available in its original version for mixed voices (ISBN 978-0-19-340551-6).

© Oxford University Press, Inc. 1970. Assigned to Oxford University Press 2010. This arrangement © 2021.

9
p
look - - - ing. God be in my mouth
p
look - - - ing. God be in my mouth
p
look - - ing, my look - ing. God be in my mouth
p
look - ing, my look - ing. God be in my mouth
p
13
mf
p
and in my speak - - - - ing. God be
mf
p
and in my speak - - - ing. God be
mf
p
and in my speak - - - ing. God be
mf
p
and in my speak - - - ing. God be
mf
p

17
Poco meno mosso
in mine heart and in my think - ing.
in mine heart and in my think - ing. God be
pp
in mine heart and in my think - ing. God be
in mine heart and in my think - ing. God be
Poco meno mosso
21
and in my de - part - ing.
at my end and in my de - part - ing.
at my end and in my de - part - ing.
at my end and in my de - part - ing.
rit.

Lead, kindly Light

Words by John Henry Newman (1801–90)

JOHN RUTTER

© Collegium Music Publications 2020. This arrangement © 2022. Exclusively licensed worldwide to Oxford University Press.

11
p
mp
cresc.
on. Keep thou my feet; I do not ask to see The dis-tant
on. Keep_ thou, keep thou my feet; I do not ask to see The dis-tant
on. Keep_ thou, keep_ thou my feet;_ I do not ask to see The dis-tant
on. Keep_ thou my feet; I do not ask to see The dis-tant
16
mf
rit. al fine
pp
scene; one step e - nough for me._
scene;_ one step e - nough for me, e - nough for me._
scene; one_ step e - nough_ for me, e - nough for me._
scene; one_ step e - nough for me, for me.

Nativity Carol

Words and music by
JOHN RUTTER

* The signs ⌐ ¬ denote the melody line, when it is not in the top voice.

Also available in its original version for mixed voices (ISBN 978-0-19-340571-4).

© Oxford University Press 1967. This arrangement © 2022.

12(68)
A
pp cresc. poco a poco
light of star He who loved us so.
babe so rare, Hearts with warmth he fills.
Far a -
light of star He who loved us so.
babe so rare, Hearts with warmth he fills.
Far a -
light of star He who loved us so.
babe so rare, Hearts with his warmth he fills.
Far a -
light of star He who loved us so.
babe so rare, Hearts with warmth he fills.
Far a -
A
pp cresc.
18(74)
sempre cresc.
- way si - lent lay, Born to - day, your hom - age
- way si - lent lay, Born to - day, your hom - age
- way si - lent he lay, Born to - day, your hom - age
- way si - lent lay, Born to - day, your hom - age
poco a poco
sempre cresc.

(Small notes for organ only)

36
p
Ov - er her son so dear An - gel hosts
p
Ov - er her son so dear An - gel hosts
lul - la - by;
lul - la - by;
42
pp cresc. poco a poco
fill the sky. (Hum)
pp cresc. poco a poco
fill the sky. (Hum)
pp cresc. poco a poco
Far a - way si - lent he lay,
pp cresc. poco a poco
Hum
pp

48
sempre cresc.
f
dim.
For Christ is born for
sempre cresc.
f
dim.
For Christ is born for
sempre cresc.
f
dim.
Born to - day, your hom - age pay; Christ is born for
sempre cresc.
f
dim.
Christ is born for
mp
cresc.
mf
dim.
54
C
1.
2.
p
aye, (Hum) Day.
p
aye, (Hum) Day.
p
aye, Born on Christ - mas Day. Day.
p
aye, (Hum) Day.
C
1.
2.
mp
p Sw. strings

88
D
pp espress. e dolce
4. Love in that sta - ble was born In - to our hearts to flow;
pp espress. e dolce
4. Love in that sta - ble was born In - to our hearts to flow;
pp espress. e dolce
4. Love in that sta - ble was born In - to our hearts to flow;
pp espress. e dolce
4. Love in that sta - ble was born In - to our hearts to flow;
D
pp
94
p
In - no - cent dream - ing babe, Make me thy love to know. Far a -
p
In - no - cent dream - ing babe, Make me thy love to know. Far a -
In - no - cent dream - ing babe, Make me thy love to know.
In - no - cent dream - ing babe, Make me thy love to know.

100
cresc. poco a poco
sempre cresc.
-way si-lent lay, To - day your hom - age
cresc. poco a poco
sempre cresc.
-way si-lent lay, To - day your hom - age
pp cresc. poco a poco
sempre cresc.
Far a - way si-lent he lay, Born to - day, your hom - age
pp cresc. poco a poco
sempre cresc.
Far a - way si-lent he lay, Born to - day, your hom - age
cresc. poco a poco
sempre cresc.
107
f
mp
p
dim.
rit.
pp
pay; Christ is born for aye, Born on Christ - mas Day.
f
mp
p
dim.
pp
pay; Christ is born for aye, Born on Christ - mas Day.
f
p
dim.
pp
pay; Born on Christ - mas Day.
f
p
dim.
pp
pay; Born on Christ - mas Day.
rit.
mf
p
pp

O waly, waly

(The water is wide)

Somerset folk-song
arranged by
JOHN RUTTER

*The original version of this arrangement, for mixed voices, is also published (ISBN 978-0-19-351351-8).

© Oxford University Press 1978. This arrangement © 2022.

12
mp
mp
mf
flow'rs both fine and_ gay, A - gath-'ring_ flow'rs both red and_
p
mp
mf
15
p
f
3. I leaned my
p
f
3. I leaned my
mp espress.
blue, I lit - tle thought what love can_ do.
p
mp espress.
f

18
back up a-gainst some oak Think-ing that it was a trust-y
back up a-gainst some oak Think-ing that it was a trust-y
f
3. I leaned up a-gainst some oak Think - ing that it was a
f
3. I leaned up a-gainst some oak Think - ing that it was a
21
mp
tree; But first it bend - ed and then it broke; And so did
mp
tree; But first it bend - ed, broke; And so did
mp
trust-y tree; First it bend - ed, broke;
mp
trust-y tree; First it bend - ed, broke;
mp

24
mf
p
legato
my false love to me. Hum
mf
mp dolce
my false love to me. 4. A ship there is and she sails the
mf
p
legato
my false love to me. Hum
mf
p
my false love to me. Hum
mf
p
mp dolce
28
(stagger breathing)
mp
sea, She's load-ed deep as deep can be, But not so
mp

*The solo line from here to the end is shown an octave higher than sounding pitch.

38
fine, And love's a jew - el while it is new, But when it is
mp
cresc.
mp
cresc.
mp
cresc.
mp
cresc.
mp
41
old it grow-eth_ cold, And fades a - way like morn-ing_ dew.
pp
p dim.
pp
Hum
p dim.
pp
Hum
p dim.
pp
Hum
p dim.
pp
Hum
p dim.
pp

in memoriam Edward T. Chapman

The Lord bless you and keep you

Numbers 6: 24

JOHN RUTTER

Also available in its original version for mixed voices (ISBN 978-0-19-340571-4), and in a two-part version with an accompaniment for piano (ISBN 978-0-19-341521-6).

© Oxford University Press 1981 and 2017. This arrangement © 2022.

10
p dolce sempre
1
T.
you. The Lord bless you and keep you: The
2
you. The Lord bless you and keep you: The
1
B.
The Lord bless you and keep you: The
2
The Lord bless you and keep you: The
13
mp
Lord make his face to shine up-on you, to shine up-on you and be
Lord make his face to shine up-on you, to shine up-on you and be
Lord make his face to shine up-on you, to shine up-on you and be
Lord make his face to shine up-on you, to shine up-on you and be

* The signs ⌐ ¬ denote the melody line, when it is not in the top voice.

22
mp cresc.
mf
The Lord lift up the light of his
mp cresc.
mf
The Lord lift up the light of his
- on you,
- on you,
mp
cresc.
mf
25
mp
coun - te-nance up - on you and give you
mp
coun - te-nance up - on you and give you
mp

28
dim.
p
peace,
dim.
p
peace,
p
and give you peace,
dim.
p
and give you peace,
dim.
p
dim.
31
pp
and give you peace,
p
and give you
pp
and give you peace,
p
and give you
pp
and give you peace,
p
and give you
pp
and give you peace,
p
and give you
pp

34
poco rit.
a tempo
peace.
peace.
mp
peace. A - - - - - men,
mp
peace. A - - - - - men,
poco rit.
a tempo
(Ch.)
cresc.
mp
37
f
a - - -
mf
f
A - - - - men, a - - men,
mf
f
a - men, a - - -
cresc.
mf
f
a - men, a - men, a - - -
Sw.
cresc.
mf cresc.
f

40
mf
mp
- men, a - - men, a - - - men,
a - men, a - - men, a - men, a - -
- - - men, a - - - men, a - -
- - - - men, a - men,
mf dim.
p
rall.
molto rall.
13
p dim.
pp
a - men, a - - - - men.
- - - men, a - - - - men.
- - - men, a - - - - men.
a - - - - - - - - men.
dim.

When the saints go marching in

American traditional song
arranged by **JOHN RUTTER**

This arrangement is also available in its original version, for mixed voices (ISBN 978-0-19-343151-5).

© Oxford University Press 1990. This arrangement © 2022.

10
BASSES 1 and 2
unis. mf
A
Oh, when the saints go march-ing in, Oh, when the
15
saints go march - ing in: Oh, Lord, I want to be in that
21
TENORS 1 and 2
unis. mf
T.
And when the
B.
num-ber, When the saints go march - ing in.
27
B
re - - ve-la-tion comes, And when the re - ve -
p
When the re - ve - la - tion comes, The re - ve -
B
Cl.

32
-la - tion comes: Oh, Lord, I want to be in that
mp
-la - tion, re - ve - la - tion comes: Oh, Lord, I want to
37
num-ber, When the re - ve - la - tion comes.
be in that num-ber, When the re - ve - la - tion comes.
42
C
1 T. 2
(2nd TENORS) mf
Oh, when the new world is re - vealed,
mf
1 B. 2
Oh, when the new world is re - vealed, Oh, when the
mp
When the new world is re - vealed, The
C
Tbn

47
When the new world is re - vealed, is re - vealed, Oh, Lord, I want to
new world is re - vealed, Oh, Lord, I want to
mf
new world is re - vealed, I want to be, Oh, Lord, I want to
52
be in that num-ber, When the new world is re - vealed.
be in that num-ber, When the new world is re - vealed.
be in that num-ber, When the new world is re - vealed.

58
(1st TENORS)
mf
D
cresc.
Oh, when they gath - er round the throne, Oh, when they gath - er
Oh, when they gath - er round the throne, Oh, when they gath - er
Oh, when they gath - er round the throne, Oh, when they gath - er
Oh, when they gath - er round the throne, Oh, when they gath - er
D
(+Cl. and Tbn.)
cresc.
64
f
round the throne, Lord, Oh, Lord, I want to be in that num-ber,
round the throne, Oh Lord, Oh, Lord, I want to be in that num-ber,
round the throne, Oh Lord, Oh, Lord, I want to be in that num-ber,
round the throne, Oh Lord, Oh, Lord, I want to be in that num-ber,
f

70
When they gath - er round the throne.
When they gath - er round the throne.
When they gath - er round the throne.
When they gath - er round the throne.
75
E
mf brightly
Hal - le - lu-jah, bro-thers, Hal - le - lu-jah, sis-ters! Hear the mu-sic go-ing
mf brightly
Hal - le - lu-jah, bro-thers, Hal - le - lu-jah, sis-ters! Hear the mu-sic go-ing
E
mf

81
round and a - round, While the saints go march - ing up in - to glo - ry, Oh,
round and a - round, While the saints go march - ing up in - to glo - ry, Oh,
87
F
mf
hear those an - gel trum - pets sound! Hal - le -
mf
hear those an - gel trum - pets sound! Hal - le -
f
And when they crown
f
And when they crown
F

92
-lu-jah, bro-thers, Hal - le - lu-jah, sis-ters! Hear the mu-sic go-ing
-lu-jah, bro-thers, Hal - le - lu-jah, sis-ters! Hear the mu-sic go-ing
him King of Kings, And when they crown him King of
him King of Kings, And when they crown him King of
97
round and a-round, While the saints go march-ing up in-to glo-
round and a-round, While the saints go march-ing up in-to glo-
Kings: Oh, Lord, I want to be in that num-ber,
Kings: Oh, Lord, I want to be in that num-ber,

*Small notes are for rehearsal only. The solo parts are shown an octave higher than sounding pitch.

113
T. solo
shine, And when the sun no more will shine:
B. solo
no more will shine, And when the sun no more will shine:
T.1 T.2
(Hum)
B.1
(Hum)
B.2
(Hum)
118
Oh, Lord, I want to be in that num - ber, When the
Oh, Lord, I want to be in that num - ber, When the

123
poco rall.
sun no more will shine.
sun no more will shine.
Cl.
p
poco rall.
mp espress.
128
H Ancora meno mosso ♩ = 69
1
T.
2
1
B.
2
p
Oo
p
Oo
p
Oo
p
And when the moon has turned to
H Ancora meno mosso ♩ = 69
p

133
Oo
Oo
Oo
Oo
Oo
Oo
blood, And when the moon has turned to blood:
138
Slowly, in free tempo
p
pp
Oh, Lord, I want to be in that num - ber, When the
Oh, Lord, I want to be in that num - ber, When the
Oh, Lord, I want to be in that num- ber, that num- ber, When the
Oh, Lord, I want to be in that num- ber, that num- ber, When the
Slowly, in free tempo
pp

143
I
accel.
A tempo vivace ♩ = 104
mp
moon has turned to blood.
moon has turned to blood.
moon has turned to blood.
moon has turned to blood.
I
accel.
Cl.
mp
cresc.
A tempo vivace ♩ = 104
148
J
f
Hal - le - lu - jah, bro - thers, Hal - le - lu - jah, sis - ters!
Hal - le - lu - jah, bro - thers, Hal - le - lu - jah, sis - ters!
And on that hal - - le - lu - jah day, And on that
And on that hal - - le - lu - jah day, And on that
J
f

153
Hear the mu-sic go-ing round and a-round, While the saints go
Hear the mu-sic go-ing round and a-round, While the saints go
hal-le-lu-jah day: Oh, Lord, I want to
hal-le-lu-jah day: Oh, Lord, I want to
158
march-ing up in-to glo-ry, Oh, hear those an-gel trum-pets
march-ing up in-to glo-ry, Oh, hear those an-gel trum-pets
be in that num-ber, On that hal-le-lu-jah
be in that num-ber, On that hal-le-lu-jah

163
SOLO VOICE or SEMI-CHORUS
with audience ad lib.
f
K
Oh, when the saints go march-ing
T. 1
sound!
Oh, when the saints
T. 2
sound!
Oh, when the saints
B. 1
day.
Oh, when the saints
B. 2
day.
Oh, when the saints
K
167
in, Oh, when the saints go march - ing
go march-ing in, Lord, oh, when the saints go
go march-ing in, Lord, oh, when the saints go
go march-ing in, Lord, oh, when the saints go
go march-ing in, Lord, oh, when the saints go

171
mf
in: Oh, Lord, I want to be in that
mp cresc.
march-ing right in: Oh, Lord, I want to be, I
mp cresc.
march-ing right in: Oh, Lord, I want to be, I
mp cresc.
march-ing right in: Oh, Lord, I want to be, I
mp cresc.
march-ing right in: Oh, Lord, I want to be, I
mp cresc.
175
cresc.
f
L
num - ber, When the saints
want to be in that num - ber, Oh, when the saints,
f
want to be in that num - ber, Oh, when the saints,
f
want to be in that num - ber, Oh, when the saints,
f
want to be in that num - ber, Oh, when the saints,
L
f
Ped.

*Small notes may optionally be taken by a few high tenors.